Contents

How to Use This Study Guide

Welcome to an eight-week journey into understanding a woman's heart. Before you get started, here is some helpful information about the different elements you'll encounter within the study:

KEY VERSES AND GOALS FOR GROWTH // Review these items as you prepare for each group meeting. They reveal the focus of the study for the week, will be referenced in Kenny's video message, and will be used in the Connect with the Word personal study time.

INTRODUCTION // This is designed to introduce your study for the week. You will want to read this before your group meets so you'll better understand the topic and the context for your time together.

PERSONAL TIME: CONNECT WITH THE WORD // Complete the Connect with the Word section before each small-group meeting. Consider this section your personal Bible study for the week.

GROUP TIME: REVIEW // The first question in this section is designed to provide you with an opportunity to talk about what God has been revealing to you in your personal time with Him during the past week. The second question is an icebreaker to help you ease into the study topic for the week.

GROUP TIME: VIDEO TEACHING // This listening guide gives you an opportunity to fill in the blanks on important points as you view the video message from Kenny.

GROUP TIME: VIDEO FEEDBACK // This section is designed to facilitate follow-up discussion regarding what you heard from the video message and how you were effected.

GROUP TIME: CONNECT WITH THE GROUP // This portion of your weekly meeting will give you an opportunity to connect with the other men in your group by discussing truths from the Scriptures and the topic for the week and encouraging one another.

WRAP // This section serves as a conclusion to the group time and summarizes key points from your group meeting each week.

Can You Relate?

You probably already know how easy it is to get into a relationship with a woman, but it's not as easy to make the relationship work well. It takes energy. It demands effort. It requires education.

Want some great news? God offers help, if we choose to accept it. But there's a catch: God's man must truly connect with God's purposes before he can truly connect with his wife (or potential bride).

In the end, a God's man finds that connecting with a woman can't only be about pleasing her but about pursuing God's plan for his life. It's about following that plan faithfully and obediently. It's about seeing relationships as instruments for making you into the man God wants you to be. It's about pursuing the truth about yourself, recognizing when God (not your wife or girlfriend) is calling you to change, and then making the change for Him. It's about getting in touch with the passion and love of Jesus Christ, allowing His acceptance and forgiveness of you to produce deeper appreciation and acceptance of her. It's about becoming like Jesus Christ who was free to love, engage with, and serve others radically. He could do this because He lived for an audience of One.

This same Jesus lives in you.

Our goal in this study is to stimulate personal reflection and honest dialogue. As you work through each session, look at your own life and ask yourself some hard questions. Whether you are doing this study individually or in a group, complete honesty with yourself, with God, and with others will produce the best results.

May you experience great blessing as you risk becoming God's man in your relationship and grow in your understanding of a woman's heart.

Trust!

"I Want the Right Motive"

The foundation of true connection is trust, and trust thrives when two people feel safe with each other. A relationship becomes "unsafe" for a woman when she has to push or nag a man to get what she needs. The right motive for understanding what a woman wants is not to curry her favor, but to obey God's command to "live with [her] in an understanding way" (1 Peter 3:7, NASB). So whether you've been married for 50 years or 5, or you are single and have been dating for 5 months, class is always in session for a God's man connected to a woman.

goals for growth

☐ Expose wrong motives in my relationship with the woman in my life

☐ Adopt the right motives for pursuing change in our relationship

☐ Experience a closer relationship with Christ

KEY VERSES

He who has My commandments and keeps them is the one who loves Me. (John 14:21, NASB)

You husbands in the same way, live with your wives in an understanding way, as with someone weaker, since she is a woman; and show her honor as a fellow heir of the grace of life, so that your prayers will not be hindered. (1 Peter 3:7, NASB)

NOTES

_____

_____

_____

_____

_____

_____

_____

_____

_____

_____

_____

_____

_____

_____

_____

_____

_____

_____

CONNECT WITH THE WORD

THIS SECTION IS DESIGNED TO BE A PERSONAL BIBLE STUDY
EXPERIENCE FOR YOU TO COMPLETE BEFORE YOUR SMALL-GROUP
SESSION EACH WEEK. COME TO YOUR GROUP MEETING PREPARED
TO SHARE YOUR RESPONSES AND PERSONAL APPLICATIONS. YOU
MAY WANT TO MARK OR HIGHLIGHT ANY QUESTIONS THAT WERE
PARTICULARLY MEANINGFUL TO YOU. BEFORE YOU BEGIN YOUR
STUDY, READ THE SCRIPTURES ON PAGE 8.

1. What two commands in this text speak to the husband? Why
do you think God instructs husbands to focus on these two areas?

2. What does the command for a husband to understand his
wife imply about the way men typically approach relationships
with women?

3. What does this command imply about the way God
views women?

4. What do you think it means to "live with your [wife] in an understanding way"? What might that look like in the day to day?

5. According to 1 Peter 3:7, when should we apply this command to "live with your [wife] in an understanding way"?

6. What consequence will we experience if we do not heed this?

7. What does this passage tell you about God's heart? About His desire for your relationship with the woman in your life?

REVIEW

What are your expectations for this study?

What about learning to better connect with the woman in your life and growing in your understanding of a woman's heart most appeals to you?

VIDEO TEACHING

▶ BELOW YOU WILL FIND A LISTENING GUIDE THAT GIVES YOU AN OPPORTUNITY TO FOLLOW IMPORTANT POINTS AS YOU VIEW THE MESSAGE FROM KENNY. WE'LL UNPACK THIS INFORMATION TOGETHER AFTER THE VIDEO.

Watch video session 1: "Trust" (12:16).

Men understand how to _____ and _____ but struggle with how to _____ and _____ closeness with a woman.

The goal is an _____ _____ with the women in our lives.

The right motive for being God's man paves the way for the possibility of real _____.

Our identity should direct our _____ and lead to an _____.

IF YOU MISSED THIS WEEK'S VIDEO VISIT LIFEWAY.COM/INTIMACY TO GET CAUGHT UP.

VIDEO FEEDBACK

In the beginning of his video message, Kenny uses a wireless commercial to illustrate the measure of strength or weakness in a relationship connection.

How many bars would you say you have in your connection with the woman in your life?

Do you need to establish a connection? reestablish your connection? strengthen your connection? Or maybe you've completely lost your signal? Explain.

Kenny talks about "oneness" as it relates to how we connect with the women in our lives. Define "oneness." How would you like to experience it in your relationship?

CONNECT WITH THE GROUP

In his book *Every Man's Marriage*, Fred Stoeker shares from his relationship struggle: "I had trampled Brenda, crushing the opportunity
for oneness in our marriage. I had stampeded her concerns, stepped
on her feelings. Such trampling is sinning against [my] wife. ...

Most of us Christian men sin against our wives regularly, but
we're just too blind to see it.

While we can all agree that sin is bad, we have trouble
agreeing upon what qualifies as sin. Most of us smugly believe
that we never sin against our wives. ... Our definition of sin is far
too narrow." [1]

**1. How have you trampled the woman in your life, crushing
the opportunity for connection in your relationship?**

**2. Are you as consistent in assessing your own actions as you
are in evaluating your wife's? Explain.**

**3. Why, according to 1 Peter 3:7, might we want to pursue a
different way of relating to our wives?**

How can we cross over from intentional ignorance to the pursuit
of understanding a woman's heart? As Todd and I (Kenny) minister
to men, we do see guys trying to connect and respond appropri-
ately to their wives' needs. But the majority of guys seem to fail
for one simple reason: their motives are messed up.

**4. Why do you think our wives are many times skeptical of our
promises to change?**

5. Marriages are often plagued with the "control factor," the tendency of a husband and wife to try to dominate one another. Think about the biblical motive you should have for connecting with your wife. How might a man's obedience to God correct the control problem?

Your motives for wanting to connect with your wife may seem right and *good*—even logical in the moment. However, they can result in your wife feeling disappointed, resentful, and manipulated. Acting in the flesh won't bring lasting change. In the end, doing certain things to gain certain responses actually prevents us from deeply connecting.

6. How does having a Christ-centered motivation for connecting make deeper intimacy between husband and wife possible?

7. What aspects of your connection with the woman in your life would you like to be different? What steps will you take to realize those goals?

In *My Utmost for His Highest*, Oswald Chambers wrote, "If things are dark to me, then I may be sure there is something I will not do. Intellectual darkness comes through ignorance; spiritual darkness comes because of something I do not intend to obey."[2]

His point? We deliberately ignore certain things because becoming informed would call for changing the way we live and think.

Perhaps it's time to check our motives, to seek after being the best God's man we can possible be, and to pursue change in ourselves and in our relationship with the woman in our lives because … Jesus said.

1. Stephen Arterburn and Fred Stoeker, *Every Man's Marriage* (Colorado Springs: WaterBrook, 2001), 23-24.
2. Oswald Chambers, *My Utmost for His Highest* (New York: Dodd, Mead & Company, 1935).

WRAP

What if your focus shifted from doing the right thing for the woman in your life to doing the right thing because you are God's man? What pressure would this take off her and out of the relationship? How would that free you to pursue change in the way you relate to her? How would that free her to embrace the changes you make? It's good to want our wives' affections and approval. But connecting with them as God's man must be about winning *His* approval.

Remember these key thoughts from this week's study:
- The right motive for changing your relationship is because God calls you to treat her His way. Period.
- The wrong motive for changing your relationship is to get a response.
- We need to step up and express our desire to be God's man in our relationships with the women in our lives.
- When we let God know of our willingness to do whatever He asks or requires, He will meet us right where we are.

PRAY TOGETHER

Acceptance

"I Want to be Loved with Christ-Like Love"

Why do we hurt those we love most? Clearly, friends and strangers have their faults; but their imperfections don't directly impact our lives like the glaring shortcomings of those who live with us. We don't encounter other people's problems firsthand. Nor do we serve as their guinea pigs for creative experiments in family dysfunction. Consequently, we freely forgive other people's foibles and offer acceptance. After all, what do we have to lose? It's easy and it certainly doesn't require much character on our part.

I've (Kenny) noticed that with my wife Chrissy, things are different. When her faults bubble to the surface, I'm right there. Her life intertwines with mine, and her problems are my problems. They play out in our marriage and directly impact our ability to connect and communicate. Her weaknesses and the differences in our personalities that used to be cute before we got married morph into sources of irritation. They can even fester into resentment.

goals for growth

☐ Recognize that God loved me most when I deserved it least

☐ Reflect this same love toward the woman in my life

☐ Recommit to assuring my wife verbally of my acceptance and appreciation

KEY VERSES

God demonstrates his own love for us in this: While we were still sinners, Christ died for us. (Romans 5:8, NIV)

² At dawn he appeared again in the temple courts, where all the people gathered around him, and he sat down to teach them. ³ The teachers of the law and the Pharisees brought in a woman caught in adultery. They made her stand before the group ⁴ and said to Jesus, "Teacher, this woman was caught in the act of adultery. ⁵ In the Law Moses commanded us to stone such women. Now what do you say?" ⁶ They were using this question as a trap, in order to have a basis for accusing him. But Jesus bent down and started to write on the ground with his finger. ⁷ When they kept on questioning him, he straightened up and said to them, "If any one of you is without sin, let him be the first to throw a stone at her." ⁸ Again he stooped down and wrote on the ground. ⁹ At this, those who heard began to go away one at a time, the older ones first, until only Jesus was left, with the woman still standing there. ¹⁰ Jesus straightened up and asked her, "Woman, where are they? Has no one condemned you?" ¹¹ "No one, sir," she said. "Then neither do I condemn you," Jesus declared. "Go now and leave your life of sin." (John 8:2-11, NIV)

NOTES

CONNECT WITH THE WORD

THIS SECTION IS DESIGNED TO BE A PERSONAL BIBLE STUDY EXPERIENCE FOR YOU TO COMPLETE BEFORE YOUR SMALL-GROUP SESSION EACH WEEK. COME TO YOUR GROUP MEETING PREPARED TO SHARE YOUR RESPONSES AND PERSONAL APPLICATIONS. YOU MAY WANT TO MARK OR HIGHLIGHT ANY QUESTIONS THAT WERE PARTICULARLY MEANINGFUL TO YOU. BEFORE YOU BEGIN YOUR STUDY, READ THE SCRIPTURES ON PAGE 20.

1. What do you think the teachers of the law and the Pharisees wanted Jesus to do?

2. Was there a justification for exposing the woman's sin that made sense to her accusers? Jot down some of your insights about this.

3. To what extent was the woman's sin the real issue? What was the hidden agenda of the religious leaders?

4. Why do you think Jesus waited so long to answer?

5. What do you think of Jesus' response to their question? What message did this convey to the woman's accusers?

6. Jesus didn't ignore the woman's sin. How did He address it?

7. What effect do you think Jesus' handling of the situation might have had on the woman in the days following this scene?

REVIEW

What has the Lord revealed to you over the past week regarding
your motives for wanting to better understand the heart of the
woman in your life?

On a scale of 1 to 10, how accepting are you? Explain your
response.

1	10
Pretty judgmental and not very accepting	Totally open and accepting

VIDEO TEACHING

▶ BELOW YOU WILL FIND A LISTENING GUIDE THAT GIVES YOU AN OPPORTUNITY TO FOLLOW IMPORTANT POINTS AS YOU VIEW THE MESSAGE FROM KENNY. WE'LL UNPACK THIS INFORMATION TOGETHER AFTER THE VIDEO.

Watch video session 2: "Acceptance" (14:27).

The number one thing women say they need is _____, _____ and _____.

When we deserved it the _____, God poured out His love the _____.

Consequences of not meeting her number one need:
1. She will _____ emotionally.
2. She will find _____ _____ to get that need met.
3. She will become _____ to other temptations.

Concrete ways you can meet this need:
1. _____ her.
2. _____ with her.
3. _____ her.
4. _____ her opinion.
5. _____.
6. Be _____.
7. Spend _____.
8. _____ her.

This isn't _____ behavior, it's _____ behavior.

IF YOU MISSED THIS WEEK'S VIDEO VISIT LIFEWAY.COM/INTIMACY TO GET CAUGHT UP.

VIDEO FEEDBACK

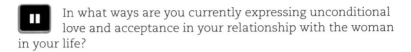 In what ways are you currently expressing unconditional love and acceptance in your relationship with the woman in your life?

Kenny lists 8 concrete ways you can fill the need for unconditional love and acceptance. On which two do you most need to work? Share with your group what you plan to do differently in these areas.

Why do you think Kenny closes his video message with the challenge to "be really brave"?

CONNECT WITH THE GROUP

As I (Kenny) look back over the years, I'm amazed. It seems I've been more likely to extend patience, forgiveness, grace, and mercy to friends and strangers than to my own wife. You call it what you will; my wife called it hurtful. The weird thing is that many times I didn't even know I was hurting her. Often I couldn't seem to help myself.

1. How do you react when your wife's faults come out?
- ☐ I magnify them.
- ☐ I withhold love until she corrects them.
- ☐ I love her in spite of her faults.

Explain your answer to the guys in your group.

2. Based on your experience and/or observation, what impact does faultfinding have on a marital relationship? Give a specific example if you can.

3. What do you think goes through a woman's mind when her husband criticizes her?

Something to consider as we begin exploring a woman's desire for acceptance is our reaction to the shortcomings of the women in our lives. How does it compare to how God responds to our short-comings and sin?

4. What fears does your wife battle? What can you do to show her unconditional love and acceptance as she struggles with her fears?

5. What impact does negativity have on a relationship? What can we do to avoid falling into that kind of mentality?

We learn much about life from our families of origin. Parents and grandparents model for us beliefs and behaviors they learned. And on and on the cycle goes. Sometimes those beliefs and behaviors are faulty, and if we act only on what we have experienced from them, our relationships will suffer.

6. Consider your family of origin and upbringing. Recall how your parents related to each other and displayed affection. What impact does their positive model or even their failures have on your relationships today?

7. What steps can you take to become more tender toward your wife?

If God were to hold husbands to the same standard of acceptance that we tend to impose on our wives, our relationship with Him would instantly incinerate. We don't deserve His acceptance, yet He loves and accepts us even though we are guilty. Faultfinding is not His style. Being God's man means it shouldn't be our style either.

WRAP

Unconditional love shows no limitations, conditions, or reservations. It is based on an attitude of complete acceptance that loves others just as they are, without insisting that they change to fit our preferences. True love allows others to grow and be all that they want to be. Unconditional love is the only kind of love that can fill us up, make us whole, and give us happiness. It's the kind of love we all seek. But it's totally contrary to our human nature to offer this type of love because it is totally selfless. In fact, it really isn't manly behavior at all—it's godly behavior.

Remember these key thoughts from this week's study:
- The number one thing women say they need is unconditional love and acceptance.
- When women say they need unconditional love and acceptance, they are saying they want to be loved with a Christ-like love.
- God loves us most when we deserve it least.
- Faultfinding isn't God's style and it shouldn't be ours either.

PRAY TOGETHER

Connection

"I Want You to Know Me Before You 'Know' Me"

Our wives want to be known emotionally before they're "known" in the biblical sense. They long to be listened to on a deep level.

Connection is a true language of love for a woman. In fact, not being listened to initiates a chain reaction in a woman's mind that goes like this: *"He doesn't listen to me. ... He doesn't care about me. ... I will find someone else who will listen to me. ... I will experience caring from that person."*

Let's face it: Most men are horrible listeners, and it kills our connection with the women in our lives. But in order to obey God and connect with them, we need to face up to our weaknesses and work on improving in those areas. It's an act of faith.

The reason many of us don't know how to communicate is because we've never seen healthy communication in action.

The good news is that a little healthy communication goes a long way. That means listening more and talking less. God has put women in our lives to help us develop a skill that we as God's men need to perfect.

goals for growth

☐ Understand what listening communicates to a woman

☐ Identify poor communication skills

☐ Learn to listen to and be present with the woman in my life

KEY VERSES

My dear brothers, take note of this: Everyone should be quick to listen, slow to speak and slow to become angry. (James 1:19, NIV)

13 The one who gives an answer before he listens—this is foolishness and disgrace for him. 14 A man's spirit can endure sickness, but who can survive a broken spirit? (Proverbs 18:13-14)

NOTES

_____

_____

_____

_____

_____

_____

_____

_____

_____

_____

_____

_____

_____

_____

_____

_____

_____

_____

CONNECT WITH THE WORD

THIS SECTION IS DESIGNED TO BE A PERSONAL BIBLE STUDY EXPERIENCE FOR YOU TO COMPLETE BEFORE YOUR SMALL-GROUP SESSION EACH WEEK. COME TO YOUR GROUP MEETING PREPARED TO SHARE YOUR RESPONSES AND PERSONAL APPLICATIONS. YOU MAY WANT TO MARK OR HIGHLIGHT ANY QUESTIONS THAT WERE PARTICULARLY MEANINGFUL TO YOU. BEFORE YOU BEGIN YOUR STUDY, READ THE SCRIPTURES ON PAGE 32.

1. What commands do you find in James 1:19? What do these commands suggest about our relationship tendencies?

2. Do you think learning to effectively listen to the woman in your life is part of God's plan for you? Why or why not?

3. What do we communicate to others when we talk too much and listen too little?

4. How do you think God uses our listening to minister to others?

5. What behavior is discouraged in Proverbs 18:13?

6. What is one possible impact our lack of listening can have on our wives (Proverbs 18:14)?

7. What negative impact does giving a verbal or even mental answer before listening have on communication?

REVIEW

What has the Lord revealed to you over the past week regarding how you communicate unconditional love and acceptance to the woman in your life?

In your opinion, what makes someone a good listener?

VIDEO TEACHING

▶ BELOW YOU WILL FIND A LISTENING GUIDE THAT GIVES YOU AN OPPORTUNITY TO FOLLOW IMPORTANT POINTS AS YOU VIEW THE MESSAGE FROM KENNY. WE'LL UNPACK THIS INFORMATION TOGETHER AFTER THE VIDEO.

Watch video session 3: "Connection" (15:08).

For women, not listening is synonymous with not _____.

A bad listener kills _____ in his marriage.

A bad listener creates _____ in his marriage.

A bad listener creates _____ to extramarital affairs and divorce.

Ways she will know you are listening:

_____ the things she says.

_____ and _____ versus talking into space.

_____ versus delete.

_____ versus ignore.

IF YOU MISSED THIS WEEK'S VIDEO VISIT LIFEWAY.COM/INTIMACY TO GET CAUGHT UP.

VIDEO FEEDBACK

In his video message, Kenny spends some time talking about how women interpret a lack of listening as meaning the men in their lives don't care. What steps will you take to communicate a different message the next time the woman in your life wants to talk?

Imagine that after things shut down and the kids are in bed, you ask your wife to tell you about her day, giving her your undivided attention for as long as she wants. How might your relationship change as a result of such focused consideration?

CONNECT WITH THE GROUP

When you're dating, you can't drink in enough conversation. You love listening to every thought, every hope, and all of her deepest dreams. Every opinion is a lovely thread in the tapestry she is weaving around your heart. But then things change …

When the honeymoon is over and differences follow us home, our wives' opinions start to feel like binding cords threatening to choke our freedom and disrupt the peace. No guy would ever envision tuning out his lover before the wedding day; but in apartments, townhomes, condos, and homes across the fruited plain, countless men are snuffing out the voices of wives seeking to express their views.

1. Do you tend to make room for your wife's thoughts or do you snuff them out? Explain.

2. Why do you think it's wrong to dismiss her voice and feelings?

3. In what ways can you relate to the ideas of communicating and listening being different before and after the wedding?

Sometimes a look into the dynamics of someone else's struggle sheds light on our own tendencies. Consider Rene and Paul. Rene says she's an open person who finds it easy to share her feelings. Her husband, Paul, is a more private individual who shares few thoughts with other people, especially in Sunday school.

Once as the couple traveled home from church, Paul asked, "Why did you have to bring up our kids again in class, Rene? Do you have to talk so much?"

Inwardly, Rene winced with embarrassment that once again her husband had asked her to keep a lid on it. *It must be something about me as a person that he doesn't like*, she thought.

4. Why do you think men tend to invalidate the emotions of the women in their lives by shutting down conversation or avoiding it altogether? What fear might this reveal?

5. How does being a good listener contribute to healthy masculinity?

6. Do you think your wife feels as if she has a significant voice in your life? Explain.

Most of your wife's gifts will be expressed through her thoughts and opinions. Her voice is the vehicle through which we husbands will be blessed, so stripping her of her voice renders many of her God-given gifts useless.

7. How might a significant increase in listening to your wife and engaging her opinion impact your relationship? Your life?

Think about the obstacles preventing you from being a man who's "quick to listen and slow to speak." And ask God to help you understand and honor your wife by becoming a better listener.

WRAP

What does it mean to *really* listen? Marriage expert Gary Oliver defines it this way: "Listening means that when another person is speaking, you are not thinking about what you are going to say when the other person stops talking. Listening is choosing to be present."[1]

The problem many of us face is that we're expert fakers. We can pretend to be present. We can maintain eye contact. We can smile. But our minds are focused on something else.

We anticipate where the conversation is going and rush to beat the woman in our life to her own conclusions. Or we start mentally rehearsing our responses and coming up with solutions before we've allowed her to finish her story. Or we just plain interrupt.

All of these modes of communication are unhealthy and disconnect us from the women in our lives. We know when somebody's not listening to us—and so do our wives.

Remember these key thoughts from this week's study:
- Intimacy for men is spelled s-e-x. Intimacy for women is spelled t-a-l-k.
- Women want to be known emotionally before they're known physically.
- Satan loves a God's man who is a bad listener.
- Hearing is a biological phenomenon. Listening is an acquired skill that helps us connect meaningfully with people.
- Men tend to compartmentalize emotions. Women experience emotions as intricately connected to every other aspect of their lives.

PRAY TOGETHER

1. Gary Oliver, *Growing a Christ-Centered Marriage* (Promise Keepers marriage seminar, John Brown University, Siloam Springs, AR. September 11, 2003).

Headship

"I Want Spiritual Leadership"

As a men's pastor, I (Kenny) wind up getting lots of feedback from wives. What keeps surfacing? The desire to see husbands step up the spiritual leadership. Wives express fatigue and frustration as they do a job in their homes they know is not theirs, yet falls to them by default.

Women long to be led spiritually. I've never been approached by a woman who said, "I sure wish my husband would notch it back a little on the spiritual stuff." That's because God has given husbands the responsibility for spiritual leadership. In order to achieve God's purposes in this area, spiritual leadership calls for submission among equals much the same way the Son submitted to the Father to carry out the plan of salvation (see Ephesians 5:21).

Submission to God, mutual submission to each other, and a wife's willing submission to her husband are all means of serving God. All are done by choice, not by force. They deepen connection instead of creating distance. When done in alignment with God's purposes, submitting makes everything else in the marriage relationship richer and more meaningful.

goals for growth

☐ Take responsibility for building a strong, personal spiritual life

☐ Promote and support spiritual values and actions in my marriage and family

☐ Encourage the spiritual gifts, pursuits, and dreams of the woman in my life

KEY VERSES

I want you to realize that the head of every man is Christ, and the head of the woman is man, and the head of Christ is God.
(1 Corinthians 11:3, NIV)

[21] Submitting to one another in the fear of Christ. ... [25] Husbands, love your wives, just as Christ loved the church and gave Himself for her [26] to make her holy, cleansing her with the washing of water by the word. [27] He did this to present the church to Himself in splendor, without spot or wrinkle or anything like that, but holy and blameless. [28] In the same way, husbands are to love their wives as their own bodies. He who loves his wife loves himself. [29] For no one ever hates his own flesh but provides and cares for it, just as Christ does for the church, [30] since we are members of His body. [31] For this reason a man will leave his father and mother and be joined to his wife, and the two will become one flesh. [32] This mystery is profound, but I am talking about Christ and the church. [33] To sum up, each one of you is to love his wife as himself, and the wife is to respect her husband.
(Ephesians 5:21, 25-33)

NOTES

_____

_____

_____

_____

_____

_____

_____

_____

_____

_____

_____

_____

_____

_____

_____

_____

_____

_____

_____

_____

CONNECT WITH THE WORD

THIS SECTION IS DESIGNED TO BE A PERSONAL BIBLE STUDY
EXPERIENCE FOR YOU TO COMPLETE BEFORE YOUR SMALL-GROUP
SESSION EACH WEEK. COME TO YOUR GROUP MEETING PREPARED
TO SHARE YOUR RESPONSES AND PERSONAL APPLICATIONS. YOU
MAY WANT TO MARK OR HIGHLIGHT ANY QUESTIONS THAT WERE
PARTICULARLY MEANINGFUL TO YOU. BEFORE YOU BEGIN YOUR
STUDY, READ THE SCRIPTURES ON PAGE 44.

1. According to 1 Corinthians 11:3, to whom is the man responsible?

2. Why do you think God emphasized the man's submission to Him before assigning the man a position of spiritual leadership in marriage?

3. What happens when men don't follow God's leadership sequence?

4. What purpose did Jesus' submission to His Father serve during His earthly ministry? What did He model for us that we can apply to our marriages?

5. In your own words, compare the spiritual relationship between Christ and the church with the human relationship between husband and wife.

6. How, according to Ephesians 5:25, are spiritual love and leadership expressed?

7. Review Ephesians 5:26-27. Why did Jesus give Himself for the church? How does His example apply to you as a husband (v. 28)?

REVIEW

What has the Lord revealed to you over the past week regarding how well you listen to the woman in your life?

Who do you consider a strong spiritual leader? What characteristics does this person possess?

VIDEO TEACHING

▶ BELOW YOU WILL FIND A LISTENING GUIDE THAT GIVES YOU AN OPPORTUNITY TO FOLLOW IMPORTANT POINTS AS YOU VIEW THE MESSAGE FROM KENNY. WE'LL UNPACK THIS INFORMATION TOGETHER AFTER THE VIDEO.

Watch video session 4: "Headship" (13:14).

Women want _____ _____ with their husbands.

Women want _____ _____.

A woman feels there is spiritual intimacy when the man …
  owns his own spiritual _____.
  spiritually _____.
  participates in spiritual _____.
  brings spiritual _____, _____, and _____ into discussions.
  supports strong spiritual _____, _____, and _____.

Women want a man with a strong _____ _____.

_____ you lead provides the integrity to support the fact _____ you lead.

IF YOU MISSED THIS WEEK'S VIDEO VISIT LIFEWAY.COM/INTIMACY TO GET CAUGHT UP.

VIDEO FEEDBACK

Kenny closes his video message with this interpretation of Mark 10:42-45: "Culture leads out of position. You lead out of service and sacrifice." If this is the measuring stick by which we gauge how we are doing as spiritual leaders, how do you think you measure up? Explain.

How has your walk with God—or the lack thereof—affected your ability to provide spiritual leadership?

CONNECT WITH THE GROUP

As husbands, we need to ask ourselves two key questions: *What are my wife's spiritual needs?* and *How do I meet them?*

Early in my (Kenny) marriage to Chrissy, I had no clue how to serve and lead out of sacrificial love. It was all about me and what I was doing; she was simply along for the ride. I had my spiritual life, and she had hers. We were independent rather than inter-dependent. We prayed together, but our prayers were superficial (saying grace over meals, for example). We weren't connected in the most important way of all: spiritually.

1. Does your wife see you as the spiritual leader in your marriage? Why or why not?

2. To what extent does your wife trust your walk with Christ? How do you know? How has this impacted her level of trust in your leadership in other aspects of your relationship?

3. Was your own father the head of your household? In what ways does his example of spiritual leadership—or lack thereof—affect you today?

Through the encouragement of friends and some very painful circumstances, I was prompted to change from my independent family leadership style to one requiring hands-on involvement. Basically, I had to get a spiritual spine. I had to demonstrate doing the right thing as God's man in front of my entire family.

4. Do you lead out of a heart for serving your wife? If so, give an example. If not, what is your motivation for leading?

Over time I earned credibility in Chrissy's eyes: she allowed me to speak into her life and provide direction. Today she sees that I care deeply about her and what's going on in her spirit and in our family. She trusts my judgment and counsel more than ever. But I didn't start earning her trust and cooperation with words alone. It started with quiet action.

5. In what ways, if any, do you encourage your wife to grow spiritually?

6. What is God calling you to do differently so that you can better connect with your wife's need for spiritual leadership?

Reread Ephesians 5:21, 25-33 and reflect on your responsibility as a husband. Pray for God's direction and His support of your efforts to meet your wife's need for spiritual leadership.

WRAP

Women have been filling a gap left by men for far too long. It's time we as God's men invest energy into our role as spiritual leaders. That decision will please God and in turn bless others. When we function as God's men in the role of spiritual leadership, the women we love—and who love us—will see that we care deeply about them. They will trust our judgment and counsel more than ever. But earning that trust and cooperation doesn't come with words alone. It starts with action. Over the next week, try to think of one new way you can spiritually connect with the woman in your life. Act on it, and see what happens.

Remember these key thoughts from this week's study:
- Women want spiritual leadership.
- Women want a man with a strong spiritual identity.
- *How* we lead provides the integrity to support the fact *that* we lead.
- When we fulfill our role as spiritual leaders, we earn credibility and the right to speak into the lives of the women we love.

PRAY TOGETHER

Encouragement

"I Want to Feel Special to You"

The myth we men embrace is that after the conquest, we can coast on the encouragement front. That lie shows a complete disregard for how God created women, and it kills intimacy in a relationship. When a man stops encouraging his wife and making her feel special, she feels deceived and ripped off. Over time the painful truth—that it was all a game, and she was simply a prize—begins to sink in. The result? A man loses his credibility and respect in his wife's eyes. A woman cannot be fully intimate with a man she does not respect and even resents. She didn't sign on for that. And she certainly never dreamed that's the way your relationship would be.

goals for growth

☐ Recognize that prioritizing our relationship makes my wife feel secure

☐ Learn what encourages a woman

☐ Initiate and integrate behaviors that encourage her

KEY VERSES

---

¹⁶ *May our Lord Jesus Christ himself and God our Father, who loved us and by his grace gave us eternal encouragement and good hope,* ¹⁷ *encourage your hearts and strengthen you in every good deed and word. (2 Thessalonians 2:16-17, NIV)*

¹ *LORD, You have searched me and known me.* ² *You know when I sit down and when I stand up; You understand my thoughts from far away.* ³ *You observe my travels and my rest; You are aware of all my ways.* ⁴ *Before a word is on my tongue, You know all about it, LORD.* ⁵ *You have encircled me; You have placed Your hand on me.* ⁶ *This extraordinary knowledge is beyond me. It is lofty; I am unable to reach it. (Psalm 139:1-6)*

He said about Benjamin: The LORD's beloved rests securely on Him. He shields him all day long, and he rests on His shoulders. (Deuteronomy 33:12)

Pleasant words are a honeycomb: sweet to the taste and health to the body. (Proverbs 16:24)

NOTES

_____

_____

_____

_____

_____

_____

_____

_____

_____

_____

_____

_____

_____

_____

_____

_____

_____

_____

_____

_____

CONNECT WITH THE WORD

THIS SECTION IS DESIGNED TO BE A PERSONAL BIBLE STUDY
EXPERIENCE FOR YOU TO COMPLETE BEFORE YOUR SMALL-GROUP
SESSION EACH WEEK. COME TO YOUR GROUP MEETING PREPARED
TO SHARE YOUR RESPONSES AND PERSONAL APPLICATIONS. YOU
MAY WANT TO MARK OR HIGHLIGHT ANY QUESTIONS THAT WERE
PARTICULARLY MEANINGFUL TO YOU. BEFORE YOU BEGIN YOUR
STUDY, READ THE SCRIPTURES ON PAGE 56.

1. Read Psalm 139:1-6. How did the knowledge that God
understood what makes him tick impact David?

2. Does it encourage you to know that God understands you
and your needs? Explain.

3. How aware are you of God's knowing and loving presence
with you throughout the day? What would help increase
your awareness?

4. What word describes God's people in Deuteronomy 33:12?

5. What does the fact that we as "the Lord's beloved" can rest securely on Him say about God?

6. When have you been most blessed by someone's encouraging words?

7. Read Proverbs 16:24. How do words of encouragement differ from other kinds of words?

REVIEW

What has the Lord revealed to you over the past week regarding your role as spiritual leader in your relationship with the woman in your life?

Who has served as an encourager of you? What has this person done that has been most meaningful? Be specific.

VIDEO TEACHING

▶ BELOW YOU WILL FIND A LISTENING GUIDE THAT GIVES YOU AN OPPORTUNITY TO FOLLOW IMPORTANT POINTS AS YOU VIEW THE MESSAGE FROM KENNY. WE'LL UNPACK THIS INFORMATION TOGETHER AFTER THE VIDEO.

Watch video session 5: "Encouragement" (13:43).

Men make _____ and devote _____ and _____ toward things that are important to them.

When people are going through the _____, it ceases to be _____.

A woman wants to feel _____ to you.

IF YOU MISSED THIS WEEK'S VIDEO VISIT LIFEWAY.COM/INTIMACY TO GET CAUGHT UP.

VIDEO FEEDBACK

In the beginning of his video message, Kenny talks about "conquering" and then "coasting" in our relationships with the women in our lives. He refers to this intimacy killer as an "8,000-pound King Kong."

Identify your 8,000-pound gorilla tendencies. What exactly stands in the way of you being her greatest encourager?

In what ways do you see God as your encourager? What can you do to encourage the woman in your life in a similar way?

CONNECT WITH THE GROUP

Go into any restaurant and observe the older couples dining there. Most take a small corner table, order off the menu, and then barely speak a word to each other during the entire meal. Their eyes rarely even meet. By paying close attention as they shuffle past on their way out the door, you can often see a haunting, sad look in the woman's eyes. Defeat. Acceptance. She's just playing out the string. Was this God's dream for her in marriage? For us? In premarriage class, every female eye is bright with hope and anticipation; but the later trampling of marriage by a husband disengaged brings death to those same eyes.

1. Think about your marriage. Has your wife found in you a companion or someone just going through the motions? Explain.

2. What behaviors demonstrate a desire to understand your wife? What actions demonstrate the opposite?

Sadly, the ability of men to encourage women seems to be a lost art these days. Men have abandoned the princess inside their wives and instead have embraced them as mere coworkers. As a result, women's dreams have died and their loving hearts toward their husbands have withered. Women have become so accustomed to the routine, the roles, and the repetition in their marriages that they feel about as special as the furniture.

3. Would your wife say she is a priority in your life? Why or why not? To what evidence might she point?

4. What time each day have you specifically set aside just to be with your wife? What is the purpose for your time together: to discuss the kids, to debrief your day, to enjoy each other's company?

Even at the earliest ages little girls want to feel special. My little girl is encouraged by my words, by my presence, by my time, and by my understanding her need to feel like the apple of my eye. Fast-forward 20, 30, even 40 years. Doesn't it make sense that this same girl, though all grown up, will still thrive on the man in her life making her his special focus? Will she blush when his extra effort makes her feel as if she's the only one in the room? Will her need—her dream—of feeling wanted, valued, and appreciated die? Absolutely not!

5. How often does your wife hear you brag about her? When was the last time you praised her in front of others? What did you say and to whom?

6. In general, do you build up your wife more than you tear her down? What can you do to improve in this area?

7. Three things you can do to make the woman in your life feel special and encouraged are to understand her, to spend time with her, and to offer her verbal encouragement. In which of these areas are you weakest? What steps can you take over the next week to improve?

Consider what impressed your wife most about you before you got married. Do you still impress her in this way? Kindness, patience, respect, honesty, and compassion go far in keeping a marriage healthy. So love her. Encourage her. Take steps to prove to her that the devotion and admiration she saw you demonstrate in the early years weren't just a mirage.

WRAP

Many of us grew up in families devoid of encouragement, so it's hard for us to extend it to others. Regardless of our backgrounds, however, we have received in Jesus Christ the deep and healing encouragement we need to break this destructive pattern. When we get in touch with how much God loves to encourage us, we are able to give away the same encouragement to others. We can encourage the women in our lives through understanding, time, and verbal appreciation.

So … if the princess inside the woman in your life has died, decide what you will do to bring her back to life.

Remember these key thoughts from this week's study:
- We make time and devote thought and energy toward things that are important to us.
- When we are just going through the motions, it ceases to be special.
- A woman wants to feel special to us.
- God is a constant encourager to us. His model shows us how we can do the same for the women in our lives.

PRAY TOGETHER

Friendship

"I Want 'Us'"

Sadly, many men are emotionally closer to and more authentic with their guy friends than they are with their own wives. Let's be clear: A man needs his guy friends, but God's plan is for his wife to be his number-one human confidante and a guiding influence in his life.

A man dishonors his wife by not recognizing her desire to be his confidante and a trusted source of counsel. More important, he disobeys God when he turns to friends before turning to his wife on the big issues that affect them both.

Is a paradigm shift in order?

goals for growth

☐ Understand the importance of togetherness to the woman in my life

☐ Commit to God's purpose of oneness with the woman in my life

☐ Build new connections to make her a full partner and a prized friend

KEY VERSES

¹⁸ The LORD God said, "It is not good for the man to be alone. I will
make a helper suitable for him." ¹⁹ So the LORD God formed out of
the ground every wild animal and every bird of the sky, and brought
each to the man to see what he would call it. And whatever the man
called a living creature, that was its name. ²⁰ The man gave names
to all the livestock, to the birds of the sky, and to every wild animal;
but for the man no helper was found as his complement. ²¹ So the
LORD God caused a deep sleep to come over the man, and he slept.
God took one of his ribs and closed the flesh at that place. ²² Then the
LORD God made the rib He had taken from the man into a woman and
brought her to the man. ²³ And the man said: This one, at last, is bone
of my bone and flesh of my flesh; this one will be called "woman,"
for she was taken from man. ²⁴ This is why a man leaves his father
and mother and bonds with his wife, and they become one flesh.
²⁵ Both the man and his wife were naked, yet felt no shame.
(Genesis 2:18-25)

¹⁰ Who can find a capable wife? She is far more precious than jewels.
¹¹ The heart of her husband trusts in her, and he will not lack
anything good. ¹² She rewards him with good, not evil, all the days
of her life. (Proverbs 31:10-12)

NOTES

CONNECT WITH THE WORD

THIS SECTION IS DESIGNED TO BE A PERSONAL BIBLE STUDY EXPERIENCE FOR YOU TO COMPLETE BEFORE YOUR SMALL-GROUP SESSION EACH WEEK. COME TO YOUR GROUP MEETING PREPARED TO SHARE YOUR RESPONSES AND PERSONAL APPLICATIONS. YOU MAY WANT TO MARK OR HIGHLIGHT ANY QUESTIONS THAT WERE PARTICULARLY MEANINGFUL TO YOU. BEFORE YOU BEGIN YOUR STUDY, READ THE SCRIPTURES ON PAGE 68.

1. Review Genesis 2:18. What word describes the woman's purpose in being a counterpart to the man? What does this suggest about God's assessment of Adam?

2. How, according to Genesis 2:23, does Adam view God's gift to him in Eve? What is Adam's commitment?

3. How might the absence of shame and guilt have helped Adam and Eve's relationship?

4. Do you think it's important for a man to be fully known by his wife? Why or why not? How well does your wife know you? What's the basis for your answer?

5. What value is ascribed to the wife in Proverbs 31:10?

6. According to Proverbs 31:11, what benefits does the husband of such a wife enjoy?

7. In your own words, describe the partnership illustrated in Proverbs 31:10-12.

REVIEW

What has the Lord revealed to you over the past week about behaviors you can initiate and integrate to be a better encourager to the woman in your life?

On a scale of 1 to 10, how would you rate the kind of friend you are? Explain your response.

1   10

I'm not a very   I consider
dependable   myself a faithful,
friend.   loyay trustworthy
                                                                       friend.

VIDEO TEACHING

▶ BELOW YOU WILL FIND A LISTENING GUIDE THAT GIVES YOU AN OPPORTUNITY TO FOLLOW IMPORTANT POINTS AS YOU VIEW THE MESSAGE FROM KENNY. WE'LL UNPACK THIS INFORMATION TOGETHER AFTER THE VIDEO.

Watch video session 6: "Friendship" (16:14).

The heart of a woman looks to her man and says:
"_____."

God's man dishonors God by not recognizing his wife's desire to be his _____ and his _____ _____ source of counsel.

Ways to intentionally build togetherness to keep your bond strong or rebuild a bond that has frayed:[1]

_____ togetherness:
being tuned in to each other's needs

_____ togetherness:
sharing thoughts, ideas, opinions, beliefs

_____ togetherness:
enjoying the beauty and artistry of life

_____ togetherness:
having fun and excitement as a couple

_____ togetherness:
doing everyday tasks as a team

_____ togetherness:
leaning on each other when times are hard

_____ togetherness:
bonding through physical closeness

_____ togetherness:
drawing closer to God and encouraging each other in the faith

1. Created by Steve Stephens, PhD.

> **IF YOU MISSED THIS WEEK'S VIDEO VISIT**
> LIFEWAY.COM/INTIMACY **TO GET CAUGHT UP.**

VIDEO FEEDBACK

Kenny shares 8 forms of togetherness that you can use to cultivate your friendship with your wife. Which of these areas do you most need to work on and why?

What practical actions will you take to cultivate friendship with your wife in these areas?

CONNECT WITH THE GROUP

Close friendships between guys are built on mutual love and respect, making them rare and special relationships. As a result, you're always looking for ways to encourage a prized friend. You ask him about his future and his life path. You invest in the relationship and monitor how it's going. You are protective, watch out for your friend's best interests, and confide in him. But what about the friendship you share with the woman in your life? How well do you monitor it?

1. Would your wife consider herself your confidante? Why or why not? (Give specific examples to support your response.)

2. Would you describe your style of connection with the woman in your life as independent or interdependent? Why?

Because you know your guy friend so well, you're able to bring out the best in him—and he brings out the best in you. You love him enough to tell him the truth, yet you never tear him down. You are a safe place for him to go, and he is your safe harbor.

3. To what extent do you invite the woman in your life into your private world? Do you allow her to point out shortcomings she sees in you? How do you respond when she does?

4. Do you practice spiritual accountability with your wife? Why or why not? What would spiritual accountability to your wife look like in practical terms?

5. How often do you ask for input from the woman in your life when you make decisions? If you never ask for her input, explain what holds you back.

Men naturally bond around hobbies and common interests, so it's easy for men to have a strong connection with other guys who share their enthusiasm for certain toys and hobbies. Sometimes they'll spend hours on end playing sports together or even just watching them. This type of connection, however, rarely develops easily between a man and the woman in his life. We have to work at finding shared interests, and sometimes that will require us to adopt new ones.

6. What activities do you and your wife do together?

7. Can you list your wife's dreams? If so, record them here. When was the last time you asked her to share her goals?

Consider what it might take for you to make a paradigm shift in your marriage or significant relationship to make the woman in your life a partner and a prized friend.

WRAP

It's hard to find a relationship more important to a man than the relationship with the woman in his life, but that may not always appear the case: it's just easier for a man to invest in his guy friends. Many men, then, need to learn how to express how important and significant that special female is. Sometimes that's work. Hard work. But it's that daily expression, that friendship relationship that a woman longs for most. The heart of a woman looks to her man and says, "I want us, not his or hers." This is God's design for our relationships.

Remember these key thoughts from this week's study:
- Many men are emotionally closer to and more authentic with their guy friends than they are with their own wives.
- A woman's heart desires "us."
- God's design for our relationship with the woman in our lives isn't "his" or "hers" but "us."
- We can't accidentally and emotionally manage our connection with the women in our lives.

PRAY TOGETHER

Thoughtfulness

"I Want to be Remembered by You"

I (Kenny) will never forget the first time I blew Chrissy's mind. We had just started dating, the infatuation factor was high, and the need to impress ran deep.

During one of our coffee talks, Chrissy told me about a "cute" jacket she had found at a boutique in Westwood. Unfortunately the price was too high, so she left it on the rack.

As soon as she started describing the jacket, a loud bell went off inside my head. *Be cool,* I told myself, *interested but disinterested in this little jacket.*

I needed more details. "Was it, like, denim?" You see, I was writing down the pertinent info on a binder below the table. "Bummer that jacket was so expensive," I said, and that was that.

Within two hours, however, I was in that boutique to win the day—and the heart of my green-eyed beauty. (Don't throw up.)

While Chrissy was in class, I went to her apartment and one of her roommates let me put the jacket on Chrissy's bed. When she got back from class, the "Hallelujah Chorus" broke out. At least for that day, Spider-Man got the girl.

goals for growth

☐ Learn to listen more thoughtfully to the woman in my life

☐ Actively direct my thoughts toward her

☐ Seek unplanned opportunities to bless her

KEY VERSES

"I know the plans I have for you," declares the Lord, *"plans to prosper you and not to harm you, plans to give you hope and a future." (Jeremiah 29:11, NIV)*

¹¹ *Making a vow, she pleaded, "*Lord *of Hosts, if You will take notice of Your servant's affliction, remember and not forget me, and give Your servant a son, I will give him to the* Lord *all the days of his life." ...* ¹⁹ *The next morning Elkanah and Hannah got up early to bow in worship before the* Lord. *Afterward, they returned home to Ramah. Then Elkanah was intimate with his wife Hannah, and the* Lord *remembered her. (1 Samuel 1:11,19)*

⁴⁶ *And Mary said: My soul proclaims the greatness of the Lord,* ⁴⁷ *and my spirit has rejoiced in God my Savior,* ⁴⁸ *because He has looked with favor on the humble condition of His slave. Surely, from now on all generations will call me blessed,* ⁴⁹ *because the Mighty One has done great things for me, and His name is holy. (Luke 1:46-49)*

NOTES

CONNECT WITH THE WORD

THIS SECTION IS DESIGNED TO BE A PERSONAL BIBLE STUDY EXPERIENCE FOR YOU TO COMPLETE BEFORE YOUR SMALL-GROUP SESSION EACH WEEK. COME TO YOUR GROUP MEETING PREPARED TO SHARE YOUR RESPONSES AND PERSONAL APPLICATIONS. YOU MAY WANT TO MARK OR HIGHLIGHT ANY QUESTIONS THAT WERE PARTICULARLY MEANINGFUL TO YOU. BEFORE YOU BEGIN YOUR STUDY, READ THE SCRIPTURES ON PAGE 80.

1. Read 1 Samuel 1:1-20 from your Bible. What was Hannah's deeply felt need? Why was this so important to her? What was the long-term impact of not receiving what she longed for?

2. According to 1 Samuel 1:11, what four things did Hannah ask of God? What was His response (verse 19)?

3. Read 1 Samuel 2:1 from your Bible. What impact did God's remembrance of Hannah have on her relationship with Him?

4. Using Luke 1:46-49, describe Mary's thoughts and feelings in your own words.

5. What did God do (in Mary's words) to prompt this response?

6. What might Mary's reaction to God's mindfulness of her and Hannah's "four things" tell us about the heart of a woman?

7. How can your thoughtfulness improve your wife's relationship with God?

REVIEW

What has the Lord revealed to you over the past week about how important togetherness is to the woman in your life?

Share something thoughtful someone did for you that proved significant to your life.

VIDEO TEACHING

▶ BELOW YOU WILL FIND A LISTENING GUIDE THAT GIVES YOU AN OPPORTUNITY TO FOLLOW IMPORTANT POINTS AS YOU VIEW THE MESSAGE FROM KENNY. WE'LL UNPACK THIS INFORMATION TOGETHER AFTER THE VIDEO.

Watch video session 7: "Thoughtfulness" (12:47).

To be used by God in her life, He needs your _____, your _____, and your _____.

A_____ your mission.
L_____ well.
A_____ privately.
R_____ the blessing.
M_____ _____ about God's love and plan for her.

To fulfill your mission:
   Become _____ in God's love for you.
   Become _____ of and _____
   in others—beginning with your wife.
   Aggressively _____ intelligence on your wife.
   Make taking _____ and _____
   _____ that show thoughtfulness a priority.

IF YOU MISSED THIS WEEK'S VIDEO VISIT
LIFEWAY.COM/INTIMACY TO GET CAUGHT UP.

VIDEO FEEDBACK

In the video message this week, Kenny talks about the longings and unfulfilled desires in life that "pass through [a woman's lips] as throw away observations and comments." He comments that the smart man who has his radar on is ready to grab this priceless information. How is your radar working?

Kenny also talked a good bit about how our acts of thoughtfulness toward the women in our lives can improve their relationships with God. After hearing this week's message, what new understanding did you gain about your role in helping deliver His blessings to her?

CONNECT WITH THE GROUP

What message did my actions send to Chrissy when I bought her the jacket she wanted? *He was thinking of me! He was really listening. He took mental notes. He planned creatively. He acted imaginatively. He invested time and treasure in me. He surprised me with a special treat. He was looking for a way to encourage me. He sacrificed his entire afternoon!*

Many long married men think back on their dating days and argue, *Well, that was then. This is now.* But the reality is this: If that's how she thought and felt and loved it then, that's how she thinks and feels and would enjoy similar treatment today.

1. What keeps you from showing the woman in your life thoughtfulness and consideration?

2. How might you practically show your wife consideration and thoughtfulness? (Hint: What tangibles and intangibles are important to her? What does she value most?)

3. How can you discover what is most important to your wife?

You may be asking what all this has to do with being God's man. The answer: God is endlessly thoughtful in His dealings with us. We are on His mind. He knows our hearts' desires and makes creative plans to fulfill them in His time. He surprises us with blessings. He seeks specific ways to encourage us. He sacrificed His Son for the joy of connecting with us. He lives in you and wants to bless your wife through you.

4. How do you think your wife would respond to more spontaneous acts of thoughtfulness on your part?

5. What sacrifices or changes will you need to make in order to be more thoughtful of your wife?

> Love is patient, love is kind.
> Love … is not selfish,
> It bears all things, believes all things,
> hopes all things, endures all things.
> Love never ends. (1 Corinthians 13:4-5, 7-8)

6. What will you gain in the long term from investing in your marriage through deliberate acts of thoughtfulness toward the woman in your life? What will she gain?

7. How will being more thoughtful of your wife make you a better God's man?

Pray as a group for the action each of you will take this week to be more thoughtful toward the women in your lives. Ask God to use you to encourage them. Be prepared to share at your next meeting what you did, how she responded, and how God used this exercise in your life.

WRAP

Our mission toward the women in our lives—should we choose to accept it—allows God to show them that He hasn't forgotten them and is ultimately planning blessings for them. God wants to use us as His delivery men, but we must be willing and available. We have to be on the lookout for ways to lovingly ambush the women in our lives. They are, after all, His daughters and He wants them to feel remembered by Him.

God loves thoughtfulness because it reflects His character. Are you reflecting Him in your actions toward the special woman He's placed in your life?

Remember these key thoughts from this week's study:
- Being thoughtful toward the woman in your life can improve her relationship with God.
- To be used by God in the life of the woman we love, He needs our desire, our availability, and our energy.
- God continues to show His daughters that He is aware of their hidden longings and wants to use us to be the delivery men for His surprises and blessings.
- It's really all about *God's* love and plan for her.

PRAY TOGETHER

Compassion

"I Want a Strong Man with a Soft Heart"

Many of us have learned to be boot-camp boys. We are stoic and show limited emotion. Being insensitive helps us in some environments (such as in sports and business), but it is disastrous for our relationships—especially with women. Our inability to express our emotions not only hurts us in our interactions with women but in our ability to connect with the needs of those around us. It fuels the perception that we are insensitive even though this is usually not the case. We just have a tough time identifying with the feelings of others or even expressing our own feelings. We are untrained in these areas.

Jesus displayed a full range of emotion. The Bible tells us that He was often moved with compassion by the needs and losses of those around Him. In some cases, He was even moved to tears. Jesus had a spine for doing what was right, yet He also had a heart for people. This Spirit of the same Jesus lives in God's man and is seeking expression, beginning with our relationship with the women in our lives.

goals for growth

☐ Recognize that compassion is a core character quality of God

☐ Develop this quality in my own character

☐ Practice compassion toward the woman in my life and others

KEY VERSES

Even in darkness light dawns for the upright, for the gracious and compassionate and righteous man. (Psalm 112:4, NIV)

[11] *Soon afterward He was on His way to a town called Nain. His disciples and a large crowd were traveling with Him.* [12] *Just as He neared the gate of the town, a dead man was being carried out. He was his mother's only son, and she was a widow. A large crowd from the city was also with her.* [13] *When the Lord saw her, He had compassion on her and said, "Don't cry."* [14] *Then He came up and touched the open coffin, and the pallbearers stopped. And He said, "Young man, I tell you, get up!"* [15] *The dead man sat up and began to speak, and Jesus gave him to his mother.* [16] *Then fear came over everyone, and they glorified God, saying, "A great prophet has risen among us," and "God has visited His people."* [17] *This report about Him went throughout Judea and all the vicinity.* (Luke 7:11-17)

¹¹ "A man had two sons. ¹² The younger of them said to his father, 'Father, give me the share of the estate I have coming to me.' So he distributed the assets to them. ¹³ Not many days later, the younger son gathered together all he had and traveled to a distant country, where he squandered his estate in foolish living. ¹⁴ After he had spent everything, a severe famine struck that country, and he had nothing. ¹⁵ Then he went to work for one of the citizens of that country, who sent him into his fields to feed pigs. ... ¹⁷ When he came to his senses, he said, 'How many of my father's hired hands have more than enough food, and here I am dying of hunger! ¹⁸ I'll get up, go to my father, and say to him, Father, I have sinned against heaven and in your sight. ¹⁹ I'm no longer worthy to be called your son. Make me like one of your hired hands.' ²⁰ So he got up and went to his father. But while the son was still a long way off, his father saw him and was filled with compassion. He ran, threw his arms around his neck and kissed him. *(Luke 15:11-15, 17-20)*

CONNECT WITH THE WORD

THIS SECTION IS DESIGNED TO BE A PERSONAL BIBLE STUDY EXPERIENCE FOR YOU TO COMPLETE BEFORE YOUR SMALL-GROUP SESSION EACH WEEK. COME TO YOUR GROUP MEETING PREPARED TO SHARE YOUR RESPONSES AND PERSONAL APPLICATIONS. YOU MAY WANT TO MARK OR HIGHLIGHT ANY QUESTIONS THAT WERE PARTICULARLY MEANINGFUL TO YOU. BEFORE YOU BEGIN YOUR STUDY, READ THE SCRIPTURES ON PAGES 92-93.

1. Read Luke 7:11-17. Why do you think the widow's situation was so serious for a woman of that day?

2. How did Jesus respond to the woman (Luke 7:13)? What emotional reaction did Jesus experience before speaking to her?

3. Share about a time when you needed God's compassion.

4. Read Luke 15:11-24 from your Bible. What did the younger son have to experience before coming to his senses?

5. What did Jesus want His listeners to know about His Father through this parable?

6. Look at Luke 15:20. What emotional and physical process was involved in the father's response to his son?

7. Do you think the father's overwhelmingly compassionate response matched the reaction the son expected? Why or why not?

REVIEW

What has the Lord revealed to you over the past week about seeking unplanned opportunities to bless the woman in your life?

In your own words, define *compassion*.

VIDEO TEACHING

▶ BELOW YOU WILL FIND A LISTENING GUIDE THAT GIVES YOU AN OPPORTUNITY TO FOLLOW IMPORTANT POINTS AS YOU VIEW THE MESSAGE FROM KENNY. WE'LL UNPACK THIS INFORMATION TOGETHER AFTER THE VIDEO.

Watch video session 8: "Compassion" (15:47).

If you don't do relationships right, you don't do _____ right.

If you don't do relationships right, you don't do _____ right.

The first step to becoming a strong man with a soft heart is seeing people with _____.

Your identity in Christ and relationship with Him reorders God's man emotionally to be a _____ versus _____-_____ man.

IF YOU MISSED THIS WEEK'S VIDEO VISIT
LIFEWAY.COM/INTIMACY **TO GET CAUGHT UP.**

VIDEO FEEDBACK

 In his video message, Kenny gave a long list of things that described Jesus' life:

Jesus was a man of deep convictions.
Jesus was willing to risk calling out injustice.
Jesus made hard decisions that produced rejection.
Jesus repeatedly went against the broken male culture of His day whenever compassion or God's Word demanded it.
Jesus spoke with authority.
Jesus stood against cultural injustices toward women.
Jesus was the truth.
Jesus was strong.
Jesus was a friend to the outcast.
Jesus embraced and forgave the morally unacceptable.
Jesus let what He saw with His eyes into His heart and allowed Himself to be moved.
Jesus gave dignity to those whose dignity had been taken away.
Jesus wept.
Jesus was grace.
Jesus had a tender heart.

How do you feel about being a strong man with a soft heart? Do the items on this list make that goal seem more or less attainable to you? Explain.

CONNECT WITH THE GROUP

Most men aren't trained to be compassionate. Instead, we're taught as little boys to push down or push away feelings of empathy. We're told to "be a man." All dads, for the most part, want their boys to develop a thick skin—the mental and emotional toughness required to stand up and stand out.

1. What messages were you sent as a child about being a compassionate man? In what ways do you think your father's ability—or inability—to show compassion impacts you today?

So he got up and went to his father. But while the son was still a long way off, his father saw him and was filled with compassion. He ran, threw his arms around his neck and kissed him (Luke 15:20).

2. What new light do the actions of the father when his prodigal son returned home shed on what it means to be compassionate?

3. How do you respond when your wife needs emotional support? (Think: Do I feel her pain and enter into it? Or do I avoid it and let her work things out?)

4. Based on the parable of the prodigal son, what experience should drive God's man toward a lifestyle of compassion and caring?

I (Kenny) am terrible at this business of feelings. I'm bad at identifying emotions. I don't validate emotional reasoning. I don't trust feelings, and I perceive those who do as weak in some way. I was trained to think that being emotional is weak and unmanly. This like-an-oak style is OK in many settings, but it simply doesn't work in relationships with most women. And over time it will damage or destroy our connection with them. More important, this style is inconsistent with being a serious follower of Jesus Christ.

5. Finish the following sentence: God's compassion is ...

6. What practical first steps can a man take to develop a soft heart without sacrificing a strong personality?

7. Let your imagination run free for a moment: What impact would developing Christlike compassion have on your marriage?

Thank God for His mercy and compassion toward you. Ask Him to give you eyes to see and the courage to help those who need to experience His compassion through you.

WRAP

God's character embodies the definition of compassion. God desires to free others from their suffering. He has compassion for people who are lost. He has compassion for people who repent and have a true desire to turn away from their sin. God has compassion for people who have faith in Him. God's compassion is not just talk and feelings. His compassion is full of action.

As God's men, we have to work to overcome messages of our youth and stereotypes from the world we live in. We're called to be men of compassion, starting with the significant women in our lives.

A strong man with a soft heart—that's Jesus. And that can be us as well.

Remember these key thoughts from this week's study:
- Jesus wants a man willing to sacrifice himself to bring God's compassion and strength to his marriage.
- The difference between Jesus and the other men around Him is that He processed what He saw and let it in emotionally.
- When women say they want a strong man with a soft heart, they simply want a complete man, a man able to stand strong and feel strongly.
- No matter what your model of manhood was growing up, your identity in Christ and relationship with Him reorder you emotionally to be a complete versus one-dimensional God's man.

PRAY TOGETHER

Group Covenant

As you begin this study, it is important that your group covenant together, agreeing to live out important group values. Once these values are agreed upon, your group will be on its way to experiencing true Christian community. It's very important that your group discuss these values—preferably as you begin this study.

PRIORITY: While we are in this group, we will give the group meetings priority.

PARTICIPATION: Everyone is encouraged to participate and no one dominates.

RESPECT: Everyone is given the right to his own opinions, and all questions are encouraged and respected.

CONFIDENTIALITY: Anything that is said in our meetings is never repeated outside the meeting without permission.

LIFE CHANGE: We will regularly assess our progress toward applying the "steps" to an amazing life of passionately following Christ.

CARE AND SUPPORT: Permission is given to call upon each other at any time, especially in times of crisis. The group will provide care for every member.

ACCOUNTABILITY: We agree to let the members of our group hold us accountable to commitments we make in whatever loving ways we decide upon. Unsolicited advice giving is not permitted.

EMPTY CHAIR: Our group will work together to fill the empty chair with an unchurched man.

MISSION: We agree as a group to reach out and invite others to join us and to work toward multiplication of our group to form new groups.

MINISTRY: We will encourage one another to volunteer to serve in a ministry and to support missions work by giving financially and/or personally serving.

I, _____, agree to all of the above.

Date: _____

Leader Guide

We hope the information we have provided on the following pages will better equip you to lead your study of *Intimacy: Understanding a Woman's Heart*. In addition to the general notes to help you along the way, we've included the answers for the video listening guides for each session. These may be useful to you if someone misses a session and would like to fill in the blanks.

This study is designed to cover an eight-week time frame. However, it is not unusual for a group to spend two or three meetings completing one lesson. Always go for depth over distance. And don't hesitate to adapt this study so that it truly works for you.

Note: You may consider bringing your men together before your first "official" meeting to pass out member books or just to give them an opportunity to check things out before they commit to the study. This would be a great time to show the Get Healthy Series overview (10:03) to those in attendance so they can get an introduction to the series. You will find this overview on the DVD in your Leader Kit.

SESSION 01_TRUST!

Key Verses and Goals for Growth—You'll want to review these items as you prepare for each small-group session.

Introduction—Each session begins with a narrative overview of the weekly topic. This material is designed to help you introduce the topic of study. You will want to read this before your group meets so that you'll better understand the topic and the context for your time together. For weeks 2-8, suggest that group members read this before you meet.

Personal Time: Connect with the Word—Each member of your small group should complete this section before the small-group meeting. In order for them to have the opportunity to complete this portion of the study before your week 1 meeting, ask group members to purchase their workbooks in advance or make plans to get them workbooks ahead of time.

Group Time: Review—In weeks 2-8 the first question in this section will be used to talk about what God has been revealing to group members from their time with Him during the week. In this session, however, you'll talk in more broad terms about their expectations and what most appealed to them about this study.

The second question is an icebreaker. It is intended to be non-threatening to group members so that a pattern of participation can be established early on.

Group Time: Video Teaching—Encourage group members to follow along, fill in the blanks on page 13, and take additional notes as they hear things that speak strongly to their own stories.

> Men understand how to <u>capture</u> and <u>conquer</u> but struggle with how to <u>connect</u> and <u>cultivate</u> closeness with a woman.

> The goal is an <u>uninterrupted</u> <u>connection</u> with the women in our lives.

> The right motive paves the way for the possibility of real <u>intimacy</u>.

> Our identity should direct our <u>energy</u> and lead to an <u>expression</u>.

Group Time: Video Feedback—This section is designed as follow-up to the video message. You will want to use the listening guide statements to highlight the main teaching points from the video and process with the group what they heard and how they were affected.

Group Time: Connect with the Group—In Session 01 you will talk as a group about trust and its role as the foundation for true connection with the women in your lives.

Wrap—At this point each week, you will want to close the group time in prayer. You may want to use this time to reflect on and respond to what God has done in your group during the session. Invite group members to share their personal joys and concerns. For this week, it's probably best for you to pray for the group. In coming weeks, as group members get more comfortable, consider asking for volunteers to lead the group in prayer.

SESSION 02_ACCEPTANCE

Introduction—Welcome group members back. Use the narrative overview on page 19 to introduce the topic of study for Session 02. Make sure you read this before your group meets so that you'll better understand the topic and the context for your time together.

Personal Time: Connect with the Word—Encourage the men to use this as their personal Bible study for the week.

Group Time: Review—This week you will talk about what the Lord has revealed to you over the past week regarding your motives for wanting to better understand the heart of the women in your lives. In preparation for this week's topic, you'll rate yourselves on how accepting you think you are. Continue to encourage group members to share during this time.

Group Time: Video Teaching—Encourage group members to follow along, fill in the blanks on page 25, and take additional notes as they hear things that speak strongly to their own stories.

The number one thing women say they need is <u>unconditional love</u> and <u>acceptance</u>.

When we deserved it the <u>least</u>, God poured out His love the <u>most</u>.

Consequences of not meeting her number one need:
1. She will <u>withdraw</u> emotionally.
2. She will find <u>other</u> <u>ways</u> to get that need met.
3. She will become <u>vulnerable</u> to other temptations.

Concrete ways you can meet this need:
1. <u>Encourage</u> her.
2. <u>Stand</u> with her.
3. <u>Compliment</u> her.
4. <u>Respect</u> her opinion.
5. <u>Listen</u>.
6. Be <u>tender</u>.

7. Spend <u>time</u>.
8. Serve <u>her</u>.

This isn't <u>manly</u> behavior, it's <u>godly</u> behavior.

Group Time: Connect with the Group—In Session 02 you will work on recognizing that God loved you when you deserved it least and how to best reflect that same love and acceptance toward the woman in your life.

Wrap—Consider asking for a volunteer to lead the group in prayer. Thank the Lord for loving you when you least deserved it and ask Him to help you do the same for the women in your lives.

SESSION 03_CONNECTION

Introduction—Use the overview on page 31 to introduce the topic of study for Session 03. Read this before your group meets so that you'll better understand the topic and the context.

Personal Time: Connect with the Word—Encourage the men to use this as their personal Bible study for the week.

Group Time: Review—This week you will be talking about what the Lord has revealed to you over the past week regarding how you communicate unconditional love and acceptance to the woman in your life. In preparation for this week's topic, you'll talk about what makes someone a good listener.

Group Time: Video Teaching—Encourage group members to follow along, fill in the blanks on page 37, and take additional notes as they hear things that speak strongly to their own stories.

For women, not listening is synonymous with not <u>caring</u>.

A bad listener kills <u>intimacy</u> in his marriage.

A bad listener creates <u>resentment</u> in his marriage.

A bad listener creates <u>vulnerability</u> to extramarital affairs and divorce.

Ways she will know you are listening:

> <u>Validate</u> the things she says.
>
> <u>Turn</u> and <u>face</u> versus talking into space.
>
> <u>Repeat</u> versus delete.
>
> <u>Ask</u> versus ignore.

Group Time: Connect with the Group—In Session 03 you will talk about truly connecting with the woman in you life, understanding what listening communicates, and identifying your own poor communication skills.

Wrap—Close your group time in prayer, asking God to help you connect with the women in your lives in a truly meaningful way.

SESSION 04_**HEADSHIP**

Introduction—Use the narrative overview on page 43 to help you introduce the topic of study for Session 04.

Group Time: Review—This week you will be talking about what the Lord has revealed to you over the past week regarding your listening skills with the women in your lives. In preparation for this week's topic, you'll talk about who you consider a spiritual leader and why.

Group Time: Video Teaching—Encourage group members to follow along, fill in the blanks on page 49, and take additional notes as they hear things that speak strongly to their own stories.

> Women want <u>spiritual</u> <u>intimacy</u> with their husbands.
>
> Women want <u>spiritual</u> <u>leadership</u>.
>
> A woman feels there is spiritual intimacy when the man …
>
>> owns his own spiritual <u>growth</u>.
>>
>> spiritually <u>initiates</u>.
>>
>> participates in spiritual <u>activities</u>.
>>
>> brings spiritual <u>principles</u>, <u>ideas</u>, and <u>insights</u> into discussions.
>>
>> supports strong spiritual <u>traditions</u>, <u>boundaries</u>, and <u>rules</u>.

Women want a man with a strong <u>spiritual</u> <u>identity</u>.

<u>How</u> you lead provides the integrity to support the fact <u>that</u> you lead.

Group Time: Connect with the Group—In Session 04 you will talk about taking responsibility for building a strong personal spiritual life as well as encouraging the spiritual gifts, pursuits, and dreams of the woman in your life.

Wrap—Request that a volunteer close your group time in prayer, asking God to help group members be the strong spiritual leaders their families need.

SESSION 05_ENCOURAGEMENT

Introduction—Use the narrative overview on page 55 to help you introduce the topic of study for Session 05.

Group Time: Review—This week you will be talking about what the Lord has revealed to you over the past week regarding your role as spiritual leader. In preparation for this week's topic, you'll talk about someone who has been an encourager to you.

Group Time: Video Teaching—Encourage group members to follow along, fill in the blanks on page 61, and take additional notes as they hear things that speak strongly to their own stories.

Men make <u>time</u> and devote <u>thought</u> and <u>energy</u> toward things that are important to them.

When people are going through the <u>motions</u>, it ceases to be <u>special</u>.

A woman wants to feel <u>special</u> to you.

Group Time: Connect with the Group—In Session 05 you will learn about the things that encourage a woman and begin to initiate and integrate behaviors that encourage the women in your lives.

Wrap—Request that a volunteer close your group time in prayer, asking God to help you be encouragers.

SESSION 06_FRIENDSHIP

Introduction—Use the narrative overview on page 67 to help you introduce the topic of study for Session 06.

Group Time: Review—This week you will be talking about what the Lord has revealed to you over the past week regarding behaviors you can initiate and integrate to be a better encourager to the women in your lives. In preparation for this week's topic, you'll talk about how you see yourselves as friends.

Group Time: Video Teaching—Encourage group members to follow along, fill in the blanks on page 73, and take additional notes as they hear things that speak strongly to their own stories.

The heart of a woman looks to her man and says: "I want us."

God's man dishonors God by not recognizing his wife's desire to be his confidante and his most trusted source of counsel.

Emotional togetherness
Intellectual togetherness
Aesthetic togetherness
Recreational togetherness
Work togetherness
Crisis togetherness
Sexual togetherness
Spiritual togetherness

Group Time: Connect with the Group—In Session 06 you will talk about the importance of togetherness to the women in your lives and take steps to build new connections to make them full partners and prized friends.

Wrap—Close the group in prayer, thanking God for the gift of friendship and trusting Him for the ability to carry it out well.

SESSION 07_**THOUGHTFULNESS**

Introduction—Use the narrative overview on page 79 to help you introduce the topic of study for Session 07.

Group Time: Review—This week you will be talking about what the Lord has revealed to you over the past week regarding how important togetherness is to the women in your lives. In preparation for this week's topic, you'll talk about the significance of someone being thoughtful to you.

Group Time: Video Teaching—Encourage group members to follow along, fill in the blanks on page 85, and take additional notes as they hear things that speak strongly to their own stories.

To be used by God in her life, He needs your <u>desire</u>, your <u>availability</u>, and your <u>energy</u>.

<u>Accept</u> your mission.
<u>Listen</u> well.
<u>Act</u> privately.
<u>Release</u> the blessing.
<u>Make it</u> about God's love and plan for her.

To fulfill your mission:
Become <u>secure</u> in God's love for you.
Become <u>aware</u> of and <u>interested</u> in others—
beginning with your wife.
Aggressively <u>pursue</u> intelligence on your wife.
Make taking <u>notice</u> and <u>doing</u> <u>things</u> that show
thoughtfulness a priority.

Group Time: Connect with the Group—In Session 07 you will talk about listening more thoughtfully to the women in your lives and seeking unplanned opportunities to bless them through your thoughtful actions.

Wrap—Close the group in prayer, asking God to keep you mindful of opportunities to show thoughtfulness to the women in your lives.

SESSION 08_COMPASSION

Introduction—Use the narrative overview on page 91 to help you introduce the topic of study for Session 08.

Group Time: Review—This week you'll talk about what the Lord has revealed to you in the past week regarding seeking unplanned opportunities to bless the women in your lives. In preparation for this week's topic, you'll talk about how you define compassion.

Group Time: Video Teaching—Encourage group members to follow along, fill in the blanks on page 97, and take additional notes as they hear things that speak strongly to their own stories.

> If you don't do relationships right, you don't do <u>life</u> right.

> If you don't do relationships right, you don't do <u>God</u> right.

> The first step to becoming a strong man with a soft heart is seeing people with <u>a new set of eyes</u>.

> Your identity in Christ and relationship with Him reorders God's man emotionally to be a <u>complete</u> versus <u>one-dimensional</u> man.

Group Time: Connect with the Group—In Session 08 you will talk about compassion as a core character quality of God, work on developing this quality in your own character, and practice compassion toward the women in your lives.

Also, be sure to discuss next steps with your group and encourage the men to Get In, Get Healthy, Get Strong, and Get Going. Go to LifeWay.com/Men for more help in developing your church's strategy for men.

Wrap—Ask as many group members as will to pray aloud, thanking God for this eight-week journey you have completed together. When all have prayed who wish to, close by praying that every man will leave this study feeling he has a better understanding of how to truly connect with the woman in his life.

Group Directory

Name: _____
Home Phone: _____
Mobile Phone: _____
E-mail: _____
Social Networks(s): _____

Name: _____
Home Phone: _____
Mobile Phone: _____
E-mail: _____
Social Networks(s): _____

Name: _____
Home Phone: _____
Mobile Phone: _____
E-mail: _____
Social Networks(s): _____

Name: _____
Home Phone: _____
Mobile Phone: _____
E-mail: _____
Social Networks(s): _____

Name: _____
Home Phone: _____
Mobile Phone: _____
E-mail: _____
Social Networks(s): _____

Name: _____
Home Phone: _____
Mobile Phone: _____
E-mail: _____
Social Networks(s): _____

Name: _____
Home Phone: _____
Mobile Phone: _____
E-mail: _____
Social Networks(s): _____

Name: _____
Home Phone: _____
Mobile Phone: _____
E-mail: _____
Social Networks(s): _____

Name: _____
Home Phone: _____
Mobile Phone: _____
E-mail: _____
Social Networks(s): _____

Name: _____
Home Phone: _____
Mobile Phone: _____
E-mail: _____
Social Networks(s): _____

Name: _____
Home Phone: _____
Mobile Phone: _____
E-mail: _____
Social Networks(s): _____

Name: _____
Home Phone: _____
Mobile Phone: _____
E-mail: _____
Social Networks(s): _____

Name: _____
Home Phone: _____
Mobile Phone: _____
E-mail: _____
Social Networks(s): _____

Name: _____
Home Phone: _____
Mobile Phone: _____
E-mail: _____
Social Networks(s): _____